Simply COLOR

ORANGE

Simply COLOR

ORANGE

A Crayon Box for Quilters

VANESSA CHRISTENSON
of V & Co.

Published in 2014 by Lucky Spool Media, LLC
www.luckyspool.com
info@luckyspool.com

Text © Vanessa Christenson
Editor Susanne Woods
Designer Rae Ann Spitzenberger
Illustrations Kari Vojtechovsky
Photographer © Lauren Hunt except where noted

Photographs pages 77-81 © Lucky Spool Media, LLC
Photograph page 103 © Vanessa Christenson

9 8 7 6 5 4 3 2 1

First Edition
Printed in China

Library of Congress Cataloging-in-Publication Data available upon request

ISBN 978-1-940655-09-3

LSID0017

*To my family who
supports me and loves
me unconditionally.*

CONTENTS

WELCOME TO
Simply COLOR

As a fabric designer I have to illustrate how a whole slew of colors go well together, and explain why the hues in the line were picked. Before I became a fabric designer, most of my quilts focused on one to four colors. I believe there is beauty in each color and love how different hues, tints, or shades can create a simple but elegant look when you focus on each individual color. All people view color differently and our interpretation of color depends on light and the interplay of adjacent colors and textures. In this book we will explore different shades of orange and some colors that go well with orange.

ABOUT THIS BOOK

Throughout you will notice some common terms and abbreviations used in sewing (for example, WOF is used for "width of fabric," meaning the measurement of the fabric from selvage to selvage). Another basic in quilt making is that the most common seam allowance is one quarter of an inch (or ¼").

Every quilt maker, beginner or experienced, starts the same way, picking out fabric, cutting it up, and putting it back together again to create a beautiful and loved quilt. If you are a beginner, the Lucky Spool website has a wonderful, free, downloadable PDF of quilt making basics that is a great place to start your journey.

I find beauty in the simplicity of color. I hope that I can inspire you to find that beauty as well.

COLOR THEORY OF ORANGE

Every color creates a mood and inspires emotions within us. Although how color impacts our senses and feelings can morph over time, it often has the ability to evoke strong responses.

The color orange is an uplifting and energetic color. Ranging in hue from pumpkin, to saffron, from carrot to apricot, orange carries some of the energy of red combined with the cheerfulness of yellow. Some color experts say that orange has a rejuvenating effect and invites a positive outlook on life so should be used liberally in our home décor. Because orange also stimulates the appetite (and conversation!), many restaurants use a version of orange to decorate their walls from terra cotta to lighter tints like peach.

The color orange has a fascinating history. Raw umber has orange, red and brown tones, and is largely considered to be the first pigment used in many cave paintings by man during the Neolithic period. Throughout China and India, orange is associated with wealth due to the extraction of the color from saffron, the finest and most expensive dye in all of Asia.

In quilt making, orange has been used since the 1860s. Unfortunately, the dye used to color the cotton fabric was made using a powder that contained a large amount of lead. Obviously, this made the dye a dangerous substance to work with but produced a highly saturated orange called 'cheddar' by many quilt historians. Today, orange is one of the most popular colors in quilting cotton, and is widely available in a range of solids and prints.

THE COLOR WHEEL

The color wheel helps identify why some combinations work well and some do not. For the most part, what "works" depends on the goals of your quilt design and the effect you are trying to achieve. Understanding how to create a variety of combinations will help you use the color orange in the most effective way. This color wheel serves as a tool to help you achieve your goals.

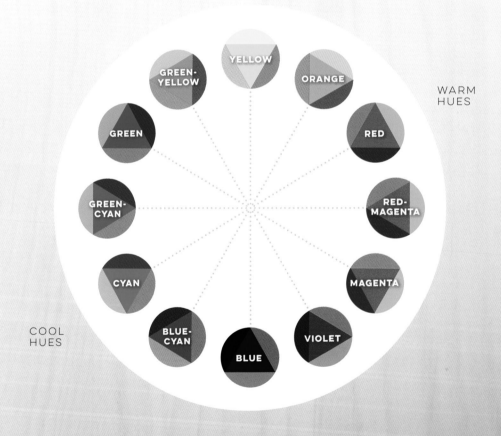

WARM HUES

COOL HUES

Hues

The hue is the pure color. Each hue has many variations, from light to dark and from intense to muted. Melon, rust, burnt sienna, and tangerine are all variations of the orange hue.

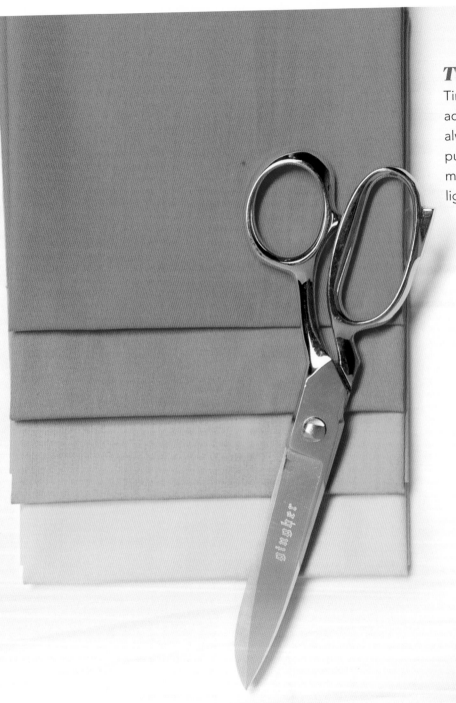

Tints

Tints are the pure hue with added white. These will always be lighter than the pure hue and have a softer, more muted feel. They are light in color value.

Shades

Shades are the pure hue with added black. These will always be darker than the pure hue and have a deeper, more saturated look. They are dark in color value.

Tones

Tones are the pure hue with added gray. Tones are muddy and can vary greatly in saturation and intensity depending on the gray used.

Value

Value is used to describe how light or dark a color is. Light value tends to include tints, and dark value tends to include shades.

Saturation

Saturation is used to describe how bright
a color is. Highly saturated fabrics have
an almost electric quality, whereas fabrics
that are low in saturation are more subtle.

Color Combinations

Looking at the color wheel, you will see that there are many possible combinations that can complement your orange quilts. My patterns tend to focus on two or three color combinations to really allow the orange to shine through, and to encourage quilters to swap in any color of their choice if they want to create a different look.

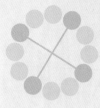

TETRAD

Tetrad is a combination that uses three additional colors that are an equal distance from each other on the wheel. For example, blue/cyan, green, and magenta form a tetrad in combination with orange.

TRIAD

Triad is created when two additional colors are selected that are an equal distance from each other on the wheel. In this case, green/cyan and violet form a triadic combination with orange.

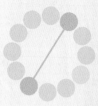

COMPLEMENTARY

The complement of a color is the one located directly opposite on the color wheel. The complementary color of orange is blue/cyan. Using only these two colors creates an intense combination, so when choosing fabrics, it is important to pay attention to the saturation levels.

SPLIT COMPLEMENTARY

A split complementary color combination is made when using one color on either side of the complementary color. For orange, the split complementary would be created using cyan and blue.

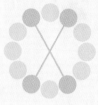

DOUBLE COMPLEMENTARY

Using orange with its complementary color, blue/cyan, then selecting a second complementary pair of colors equal distance from the original pair is called a double complementary. Orange and blue/cyan used with green/yellow and violet would create this combination.

ANALOGOUS AND MONOCHROME

Working very closely within the tints and tones of one hue creates a monochromatic design, while using orange with the colors on either side of it (yellow and red) creates an analogous grouping and using the colors on either side of those (yellow/orange and red/orange) creates a more varied, but still monochrome combination.

Interchangeable Projects

While it is important and inspiring to understand how orange interacts with other colors, I wanted the quilts and projects in this Simply Color series to be interchangeable both with each color in the series and within the individual books. Because of that, I use orange and one or two neutrals in almost all the projects. This allows you to more easily see how swapping out just one fabric can feature your favorite color. I do hope that the Color Theory section inspires you to experiment. For example, the Creamsicle (see page 32) quilt would be stunning made up using a double-complementary fabric combination.

The
PROJECTS

CREAMSICLE

This orange peel quilt was inspired by my love of petals and circles and you will love the appliqué method I use to create perfect points and curves. To make the quilt personal and fun, I switched out backgrounds to be the opposite in random places. Using leftover fabrics from my stash and inserting a few with larger prints, made the petals interesting and fun to layout. This quilt will go down as one of my favorite quilts I have ever made.

Finished Quilt Size:
72" x 72"

Finished Block Size: 9" x 9"

Materials
6 assorted Orange Prints: ¾ yard each

Linen Fabric (lighter shade): 4 yards

Linen Fabric (darker shade): 1 yard

Fusible Web at least 20" wide: 8¼ yards

Backing Fabric: 4½ yards

Binding Fabric: ¾ yard

Batting: 78" x 78"

TIP: Cut the 10" squares of each color first, then reserve the rest for the Petals. This will ensure that you get the most out of your fabric.

Cutting
See the cutting diagram on page 36 (Fig. 1)

From each Orange Print, cut:

(2) 10" squares for Background blocks

From lighter shade of Linen Fabric, cut:

(46) 10" squares for Background blocks

From darker shade of Linen Fabric, cut:

(6) 10" squares for Background blocks

From Fusible Web, cut:

(64) 9¼" squares

From Binding Fabric, cut:

(8) 2½" x WOF strips

Preparing the Petal Template

Create the Petal Template (see page 45) by enlarging and using cardboard or quilt template plastic.

Piecing the Petal Blocks

PETALS

1. Using the Petal Template and referencing Figure 1, draw nine petals on the wrong side of each of the Orange Prints.

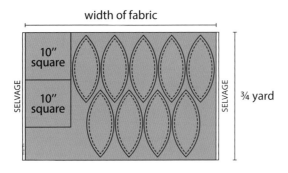

Figure 1

2. Cut at least ½" around the drawn line of each Petal (solid line in Figure 1).

3. Lay a Petal, right side down, on top of a piece of Fusible Web. The textured side of the Fusible Web should be facing the right side of the Petal fabric.

4. Stitch along one side of the Petal, beginning with a backstitch. Continue sewing on the drawn line (Fig. 2). When you reach the corner, put your needle in the needle down position, pivot, and continue sewing until you reach your starting point. Backstitch.

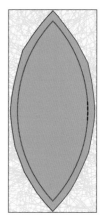

Figure 2

5. Trim around the Petal, leaving at least an ⅛" seam allowance.

> **TIP:** Trimming the Fusible Web slightly smaller than the Petal enables the seam allowance to roll slightly toward the back side of the appliqué once it is turned. This makes it easier to press and apply to your background fabric.

6. Carefully clip curved edges and clip off the two points (Fig. 3). Make sure you don't clip too closely — the stitched line must stay intact. This reduces bulk and also decreases the chance of ripping the Fusible Web when trimming.

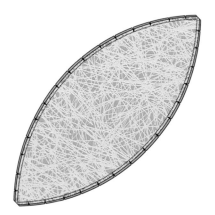

Figure 3

7. Gently pull the Fusible Web away from the fabric (Fig. 4). Make a slit in the middle of the Fusible Web and gently turn the entire Petal inside out. Use a pin to push out the points of each Petal.

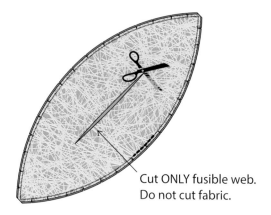

Cut ONLY fusible web. Do not cut fabric.

Figure 4

8. Group fabrics to create 46 Orange Petal/light Linen Background blocks, six Orange Petal/dark Linen Background blocks, eight light Linen Petal/Orange Background blocks, and four dark Linen Petal/Orange Background blocks. You will have a total of 64 blocks.

SQUARES

1. Working in the groups, center the Petal on the diagonal in the middle of a 10" Background block, making sure the points of the Petal are aligned with the corners of the block (Fig. 5). We will trim the block later, so just eyeballing the center is fine.

> **TIP:** Finger press the background block diagonally and align the Petal's points directly on top of the creased line. (Fig. 5)

2. Pin the Petal into place and, with your steam setting off and your iron on high, fuse the Petal to the Background fabric.

3. Appliqué by machine (using a narrow zig-zag setting) or by hand to secure the Petals in place.

> **TIP:** Using thread the same shade as your Petal will conceal your stitches. You could also use invisible thread.

4. Trim all blocks to 9½" square, making sure there is a ¼" seam allowance along the edges of both petal points. (Fig. 6)

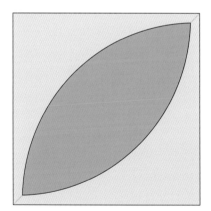

Figure 5

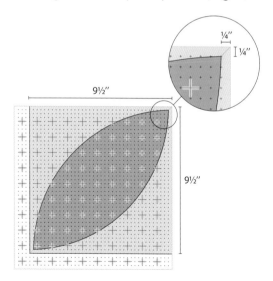

Figure 6

5. Repeat to create 46 Orange Petal/ light Linen Background blocks, six Orange Petal/dark Linen Background blocks, eight light Linen Petal/Orange Background blocks, and four dark Linen Petal/Orange Background blocks. You will have a total of 64 blocks.

Assembling the Quilt Top

1. Referencing Figure 7, arrange the blocks into eight rows of eight blocks each.

> **TIP:** It might help to use a design wall or a large floor surface to lay out all of your blocks. Be sure to rearrange the blocks as necessary to achieve a good balance of light and dark values

2. With right sides together, sew blocks into rows. Press seams open.

3. Sew rows together, pressing seams in opposite directions.

Finishing

1. Layer with the batting and backing, baste, and quilt as desired.

2. Attach the binding using your favorite method.

Figure 7

Variation
TULIP TABLE RUNNER

Finished Runner Size:
18" x 45"

Finished Block Size: 9" x 9"

Materials
10 assorted Orange Prints:
10" squares of each

Linen Fabric: 1 yard

**Fusible Web at least 20"
wide:** 1½ yards

Backing Fabric: 1½ yards

Binding Fabric: ⅓ yard

Batting: 24" x 51"

Cutting
From Linen Fabric, cut:
(10) 10" squares

From Fusible Web, cut:
(10) 9¼" squares

From Backing Fabric, cut:
(1) 24" x 51" rectangle

From Binding Fabric, cut:
(3) 2½" x WOF strips

Preparing the Petal Template

Create the Petal Template (see page 45) by enlarging and using cardboard or quilt template plastic.

Making the Blocks

1. Place the Petal Template along the diagonal of each 10'' Prints square and cut leaving at least ½'' around the Template.

2. Follow the steps from *Piecing the Petal Blocks* (see page 34) to create a total of (10) 9½" unfinished blocks using one Petal from each of the 10 Orange Prints.

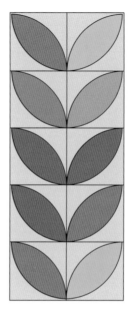

Figure 1

Assembling the Quilt Top

1. Arrange two Petal blocks with points meeting at the bottom (Fig. 1). With right sides together, sew to make a two-block set. Press seams open. Repeat to create a total of five sets.

2. Referencing Figure 1, sew the rows together into a column of five. Press seams open.

Finishing

1. Layer with the batting and backing, baste, and quilt as desired.

2. Attach the binding using your favorite method.

Creamsicle Template

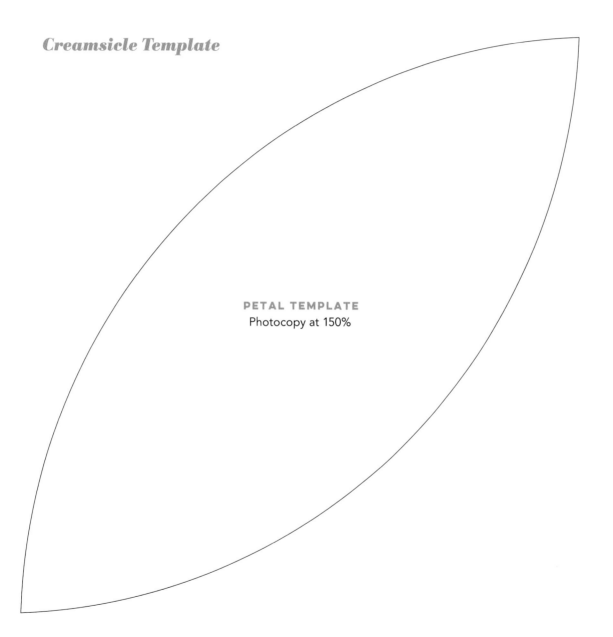

PETAL TEMPLATE
Photocopy at 150%

Orange
CRUSH

*O*range is one of those colors that can either be a wonderful complementary color or can appear harsh when placed next to the wrong color. The combination of orange and blue (true complementary colors) in this project is pleasing to the eye mostly because of the saturation levels I chose. I decided to place the blocks off-center and on top of each other to create a sort of building block look.

Finished Quilt Size:
64" x 80"

Finished Block Size:
16'' x 16''

Materials

Orange Fabric: 1½ yards

Blue Fabric: 4¾ yards

Backing Fabric: 5 yards

Binding Fabric: ¾ yard

Batting: 70" x 86"

Water-soluble pen

Clear acrylic ruler

Cutting

From Orange Fabric, cut:

(6) 5¾" x WOF strips
   Subcut (40) 5¾" squares

(3) 4½" x WOF strips
   Subcut (20) 4½" squares

From Blue Fabric, cut:

(6) 5¾" x WOF strips
   Subcut (40) 5¾" squares

(3) 4½" x WOF strips
   Subcut (20) 4½" squares

(2) 8½" x WOF strips
   Subcut (5) 8½" squares

(7) 16½" x WOF strips
   Subcut (1) 6½" x 16½" rectangle
   Subcut (1) 10½" x 16½" rectangle
   Subcut (2) 12½" x 16½" rectangles
   Subcut (1) 20½" x 16½" rectangle
   Subcut (1) 28½" x 16½" rectangle
   Subcut (2) 36½" x 16½" rectangles
   Subcut (1) 38½" x 16½" rectangle
   Subcut (1) 42½" x 16½" rectangle

From Binding Fabric, cut:

(9) 2½" x WOF strips

Piecing the Blocks
BLOCK CENTER

1. Using your water-soluble pen and a ruler, draw a diagonal line from corner to corner on the wrong side of all of the 4½" Orange squares.

2. Place two 4½" Orange squares, right sides and pin together, on opposite corners of one 8½" Blue square. Orange squares will slightly overlap in the center. (Fig. 1)

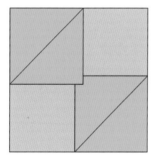

Figure 1

3. Sew on drawn lines.

4. Align the stitching with the ¼" line on the ruler and trim away the excess Blue and Orange fabric using a clear acrylic ruler leaving a ¼" seam allowance.

5. Turn the block 180 degrees and repeat for the other Orange square.

6. Press seams open. (Fig. 2)

Figure 2

7. Place two 4½" Orange squares on the other two opposite corners.

8. Sew on drawn lines. (Fig. 3)

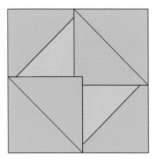

Figure 3

9. Repeat Steps 4–6.

10. Repeat Steps 2–9 to create a total of five block centers. (Fig. 4)

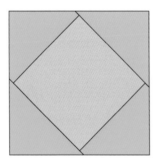

Figure 4

HOURGLASS POINTS

1. Using your water-soluble pen and a ruler, draw a diagonal line from corner to corner on the back of all the 5¾" Orange squares.

2. With right sides together and the diagonal line beginning at the top left corner, layer one 5¾" Orange square on top of one 5¾" Blue square. (Fig. 5)

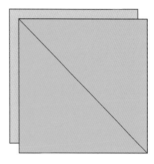

Figure 5

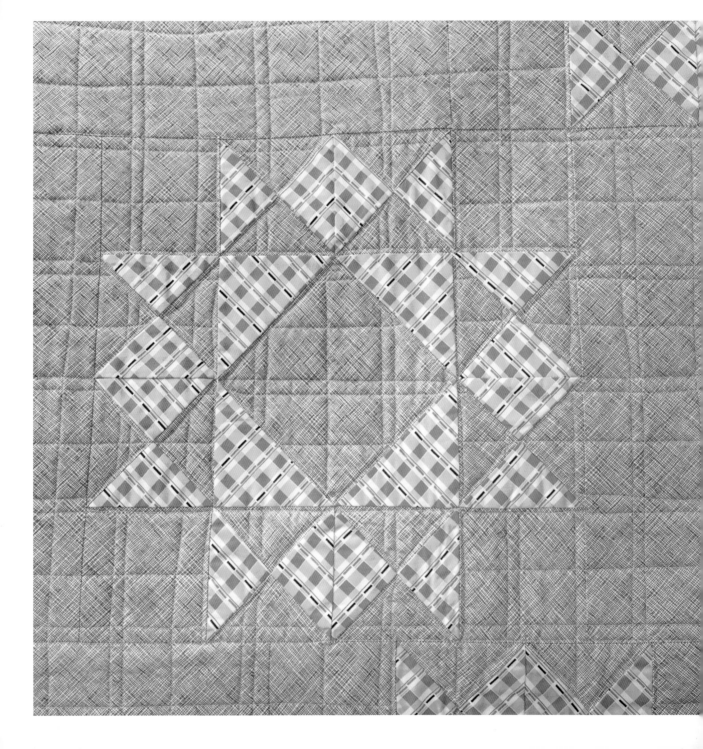

3. Sew ¼" seams on either side of the drawn line. (Fig. 6)

Figure 6

4. Cut along the drawn line to create two Half-Square Triangles (HST) units. (Fig. 7)

Figure 7

5. With right sides together, layer the two HST units so that opposite fabrics are matched (Blue with Orange, Orange with Blue).

6. Using your water-soluble pen and a ruler, draw a line diagonally from corner to corner, perpendicular to the seam.

7. Sew ¼" inch seams on either side of drawn line. (Fig. 8)

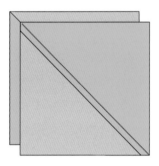

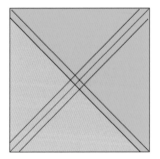

Figure 8

8. Cut along the drawn line to create two hourglass blocks.

9. Press seams open. (Fig. 9)

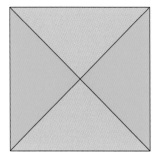

Figure 9

10. Square up the hourglass block to 4½" by aligning the center point of the block with the 2¼" mark of your acrylic ruler, then trim away the excess on each side.

> **TIP:** It would be helpful to have a square ruler with a diagonal line on it so you can line up the diagonal seam to the diagonal ruler line.

11. Repeat Steps 2–10 to create a total of eight hourglass blocks.

Assembling the Block

1. Referring to Figure 10, lay out hourglass blocks with the Blue hourglass positioned vertically.

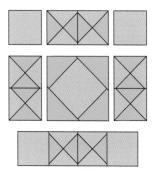

Figure 10

2. With right sides together, sew two hourglass blocks to create one hourglass unit.

3. Repeat to create a total of four sewn hourglass units. Press.

4. Lay out two sewn hourglass units on either side of the center block.

5. Sew hourglass units to the left and right side of the center block.

6. Sew together one hourglass unit between two 4½" Blue squares to create a strip unit.

7. Repeat Step 6 to make a total of two strip units. Press.

8. Pin and sew strip units at the top and bottom of the center sewn block. Press seams in opposite directions for each row so that your seams nest.

9. Repeat Steps 1–8 to create a total of five blocks.

Assembling the Quilt Top

1. Referring to Figure 11, lay out the five rows in the following order:

Row 1: (1) 6½" x 16½" Blue rectangle, (1) pieced block, (1) 42½" x 16½" Blue rectangle.

Row 2: (1) 12½" x 16½" Blue rectangle, (1) pieced block, (1) 36½" x 16½" Blue rectangle.

Row 3: (1) pieced block, (1) 12½" x 16½" Blue rectangle, (1) 36½" x 16½" Blue rectangle

Row 4: (1) 20½" x 16½" Blue rectangle, (1) pieced block, (1) 28½" x 16½" Blue rectangle

Row 5: (1) 10½" x 16½" Blue rectangle, (1) pieced block, (1) 38½" x 16½" Blue rectangle

2. With right sides together, sew blocks together to create five rows.

3. Sew rows together, pressing seams in opposite directions.

Finishing

1. Layer with the batting and backing, baste, and quilt as desired.

2. Attach the binding using your favorite method.

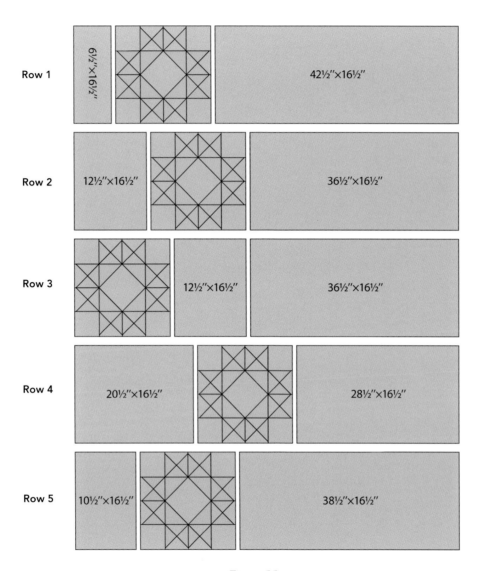

Row 1

6½"×16½"

42½"×16½"

Row 2

12½"×16½"

36½"×16½"

Row 3

12½"×16½"

36½"×16½"

Row 4

20½"×16½"

28½"×16½"

Row 5

10½"×16½"

38½"×16½"

Figure 11

Pumpkin Pie
PILLOW

*O*ne of my favorite holidays is Thanksgiving. I love the whole idea of preparing for a special meal to celebrate our blessings. Pumpkin pie is one of the special pies we make for this day and also one of my son's favorites. The orange snowball blocks represent the pumpkin pies and the number of snowballs is how many pies my son probably wishes I would make throughout the year.

Finished Pillow Size:
18" x 18"

Finished Block Size:
1½"x 1½"

Materials

Orange Fabric: 1 yard

White Fabric: ½ yard

Fusible Interfacing at least 20" wide: 1¼ yard

20" Square Pillow Insert

Cutting

From Orange Fabric, cut:

(7) 2" x WOF strips
    Subcut (144) 2" squares

(1) 18½" x 10½" rectangle
(1) 18½" x 14½" rectangle

From White Fabric, cut:

(14) 1" x WOF strips
    Subcut (576) 1" squares

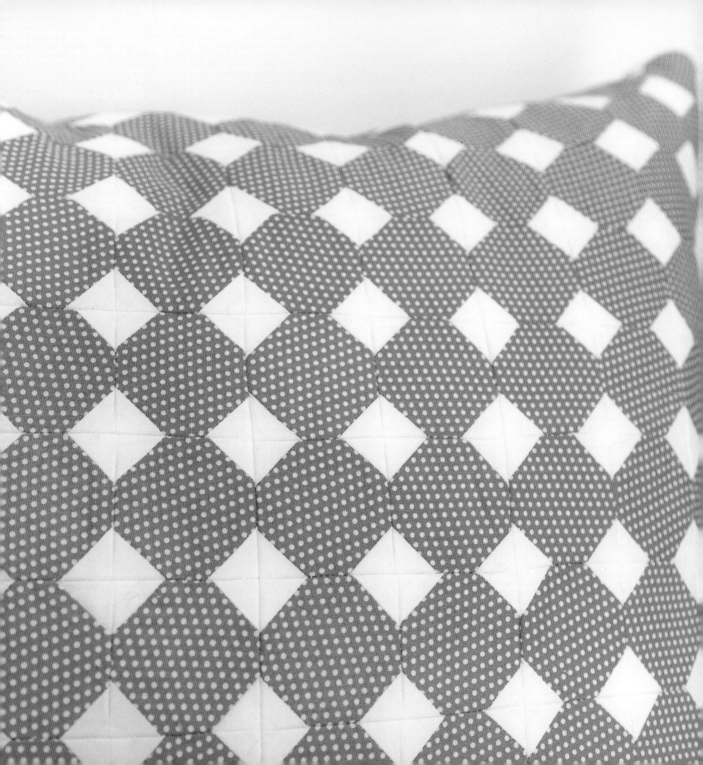

Making the Snowball Block

1. Using your water-soluble pen and a ruler, draw a diagonal line from corner to corner on each of the 576 white 1" squares.

> **TIP:** These are small enough squares that you might feel comfortable eyeballing your sewing line instead of drawing the line for all 576 squares.

2. With right sides together, place one 1" White square in top left corner of one 2" Orange square. (Fig. 1)

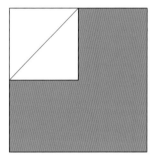

Figure 1

3. Sew on drawn line.

4. Chain-piece a White square in one corner of the remaining 143 Orange 2" squares.

5. Repeat Steps 2–4 for each corner of your Orange square. (Fig 2)

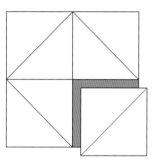

Figure 2

6. Align the stitching with the ¼" line on the ruler and trim away the excess fabric from each corner, leaving a ¼" seam. (Fig. 3)

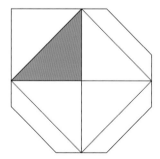

Figure 3

7. Press seams open.

Piecing the Pillow Front

1. Referring to Figure 6 (see page 64), arrange the snowballs in 12 rows of 12 blocks.

2. With right sides together, sew blocks into rows.

3. Press all seams open.

4. With right sides together, sew rows together.

5. Press seams open.

6. Following the manufacturer's instructions, fuse Interfacing to the back of your sewn pillow top. Quilt if desired.

Finishing as an Envelope-Back Slip Cover Pillow

1. Following the manufacturer's instructions, fuse Interfacing to each of the two back panel pieces.

2. Make a double hem on one long side of each of your back panel rectangles by folding one 18½" edge in ¼" and pressing with an iron. Fold edge in another ¼" and press. Topstitch ⅛" away from the folded edge. (Fig. 4)

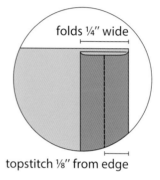

folds ¼" wide

topstitch ⅛" from edge

Figure 4

3. Lay your finished pillow front facing up. (Fig. 5)

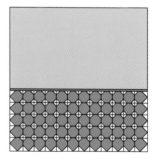

Figure 5

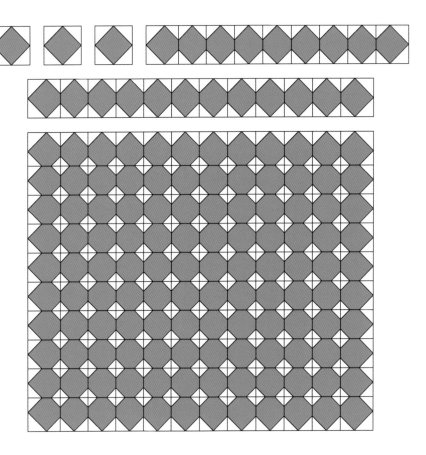

Figure 6

4. With right sides together, align one back panel rectangle with the left edge of the pillow front. Align the other back panel with the right edge of the pillow front. The back panel rectangles will overlap. (Fig. 7)

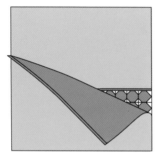

Figure 7

5. Pin around all four sides and sew using a ¼" seam. Clip away the corner points, being careful not to cut into the seam.

6. Turn inside out.

7. Place a 20" square pillow inside the pillow sleeve.

> **TIP:** When you insert a slightly larger-sized pillow than your finished sleeve, it will make your pillow more full and tight and be less likely to deflate over time.

Cheese
CRACKERS

The inspiration for this quilt was those orange crackers that we bring to school or picnics, have for a snack, or just munch on for comfort food. Cheese Crackers is the perfect name for this orange, yellow, and white quilt, with its simple design of on-point squares combined with different shades of orange and a little bit of yellow. The four large squares are made up of orange half-square triangles with an accent of yellow. The background is white to make the on-point squares (crackers) the main focal point.

Finished Quilt Size:
74" x 74"

Finished Block Size:
34'' x 34''

Materials
Dark, Medium and Light Orange, Medium Yellow Print Fabrics: ¾ yard of each

White Fabric: 2¾ yards

Orange Border Fabric: ½ yard

Backing Fabric: 4½ yards

Binding Fabric: ¾ yard

Batting: 80" x 80"

Water-soluble pen

Clear acrylic ruler

Cutting
From each of the four Prints, cut:
(7) 4" x WOF strips
 Subcut (64) 4" squares

From White Fabric, cut:
(4) 17⅞" x WOF strips
 Subcut (8) 17⅞" squares
 Subcut each square once diagonally
(8) 2½" x WOF strips

From Orange Border Fabric, cut:
(8) 1½" x WOF strips

From Binding Fabric, cut:
(8) 2½" x WOF strips

Assembling the Blocks

1. Using a water-soluble pen and a ruler, draw a diagonal line on the wrong side of 256 Prints squares. (Fig. 1)

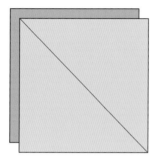

Figure 1

2. Pair up diagonally marked squares with non-marked Prints squares, mixing up the different fabric combinations to create a scrappy look.

3. On each pair of squares, stitch ¼" on either side of drawn diagonal line. (Fig. 2)

Figure 2

4. Cut on the diagonal line to create two Half-Square Triangle (HST) units. Press open. (Fig. 3)

Figure 3

5. Repeat Steps 3–4 to create a total of 512 HST units.

6. Trim all HST units to 3½" square.

> **TIP:** Use a square ruler to trim. Place the ruler's diagonal line on the diagonal sewn seam while trimming. This will help ensure that your diagonal line is perfectly in the middle of your corners.

7. Randomly place two HST units right sides together and sew. Continue chain-piecing the remaining squares, mixing up the direction of the diagonal seams on the HST units. Press open.

8. Pair up two sets of HST pairs right sides together along the long side (Fig. 4). Chain-piece to create (16) 4-Patch blocks of HST squares. Press open.

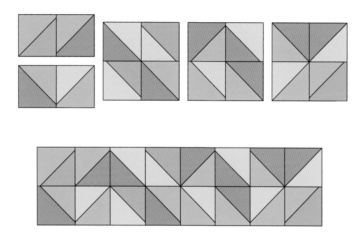

Figure 4

9. Lay out four rows of four 4-Patch blocks, rotating each as necessary to create a balanced distribution of colors. (Fig. 5)

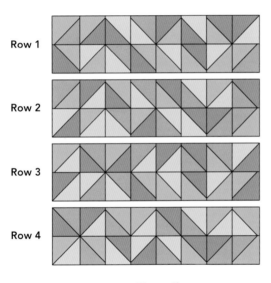

Row 1
Row 2
Row 3
Row 4

Figure 5

10. Sew Row 1 and 2 together and Row 3 and 4 together, pressing the seams open as you attach each row.

> TIP: **Number the rows, marking them with washi tape, or sticky notes, to maintain your desired sequence.**

11. Right sides together, sew Row 1/2, to Row 3/4 together. Press open.

12. Fold the White 17⅞" triangle in half along the center of the long side. Finger-press to mark the middle. Do the same for all four triangles. (Fig. 6)

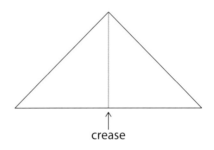

crease

Figure 6

13. Line up the finger-pressed crease and the middle of one side of the sewn square.

14. Pin in place. Sew. (Fig. 7)

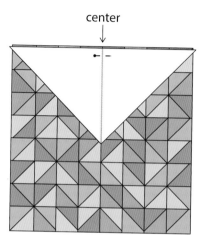

Figure 7

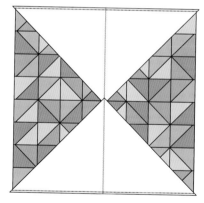

Figure 8

15. Repeat Steps 13–14 on the other side of the center square overlapping the points in the center. (Fig. 8)

16. Repeat for the remaining two sides. Press open. The block should measure approximately 34½" square, unfinished. (Fig. 9)

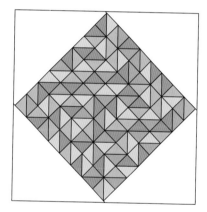

Figure 9

17. Repeat Steps 8–16 to create a total of four completed blocks.

Assembling the Quilt top

1. Lay out the quilt blocks into a large 4-patch. Sew the top two blocks together, pressing the seams open.

2. Repeat for the lower two blocks and attach the two rows together.

3. Sew two of the Orange 1½" x WOF strips together. Press seam open. Repeat for the remaining six strips to create a total of four strip pairs.

4. Attach a strip pair to the right and left sides of the large 4-Patch, pressing seams toward the border fabric and trimming the excess as necessary. (Fig. 10)

5. Repeat for the top and bottom Orange border strips.

6. Repeat Steps 2–5 for the 2½" White border strips, pressing the seams toward the Orange border fabric. (Fig. 10)

Finishing

1. Layer with the batting and backing, baste, and quilt as desired.

2. Attach the binding using your favorite method.

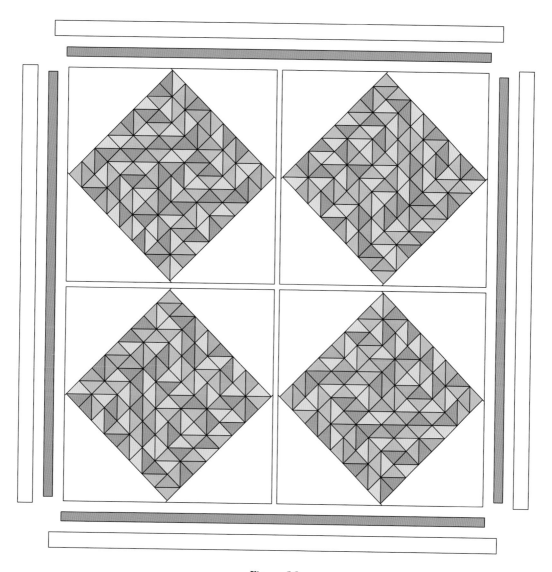

Figure 10

Sliced
PINCUSHION

*O*f course I had to include a citrus orange in the orange book! This cute orange slice can house all the pins for your sewing projects. It is the perfect size to take to a class or to look adorable on your sewing table. This slice is sure to bring a smile to your face whenever you reach for your pins and would make an ideal gift for all of the sewists in your life.

Finished Size: 6" x 3"

Materials
Orange Fabric: 10" square

Orange Felt: 9" x 2½" rectangle

Green Felt: 3" x 4" rectangle

White Felt Scrap: 2" square (at least)

Lightweight Fusible Interfacing: 10" square

White double-fold ¼"-wide Bias Tape: 18"

Brown single-fold ½"-wide Bias Tape: 10"

Water-soluble pen

White thread

Brown thread

Light green Embroidery Floss

Polyfill

Cutting
From Orange Felt, cut:
(1) using Peel Template (see page 86)

From Green Felt, cut:
(1) using Leaf Template (see page 87)

From White Felt, cut:
(1) using Circle Template (see page 86)

Assembling the Orange Slice

1. Following the manufacturer's instructions, fuse Interfacing to the wrong side of the Orange fabric.

2. Using the Slice Template (see page 87), cut two slices from the interfaced Orange fabric.

3. Using a water-soluble pen and a ruler, transfer the segment lines to each slice.

4. Using White thread in your machine, stitch over each drawn line three times. (Fig. 1)

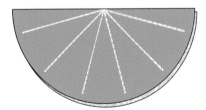

Figure 1

5. Using the Circle Template (see page 86), cut one circle from the White felt scrap. Cut in half to create two half-circles.

6. Place one White felt half-circle on the orange slice as indicated on the Slice Template (see page 87). Using White thread in your machine, sew the half-circle to the slice. Stitch as close to the edge of the felt as possible. (Fig. 2)

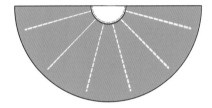

Figure 2

7. Repeat for the second Orange fabric slice.

Assembling the Pincushion

1. With right sides together and beginning ¼" from the edge, stitch the two slices together along the top edge. Stop stitching ¼" before you reach the end of the slices. Press seams open.

2. Beginning at the seam line and approximately ½" from the joined slice seam, place the White bias tape ¼" inside the outer edge of the entire circumference of the joined Orange slices (Fig. 3). Pin in place. Where the bias tape meets, fold one end under by ¼". Tuck the raw end under the folded end.

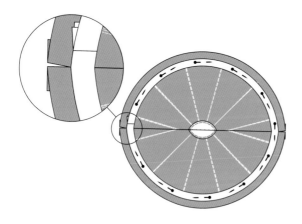

Figure 3

> TIP: It can be tricky to work with narrow bias tape. The leaf will be placed over the area where the bias tape meets, so perfection is not required!

3. Edgestitch along both sides of the bias tape to secure in place (Fig. 4). Set aside.

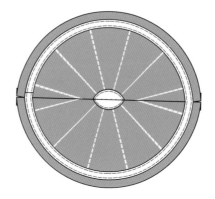

Figure 4

4. Fold the Brown bias tape with right sides together and edgestitch along both sides (I used a matching Brown thread).

5. Fold sewn Brown bias tape in half to form a loop. Attach raw edges ½" down from the center seam on one side of the orange slice, using the placement diagram shown on the Slice Template. Matching the raw edges, secure in place by stitching ⅛" from the raw edge. (Fig. 5)

6. With right sides together and with the loop inside the gusset, pin or clip one edge of the Orange felt peel piece to one edge of the slice. (Fig. 6)

Figure 6

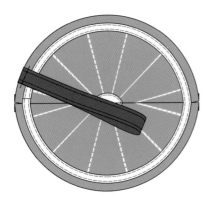

Figure 5

7. Beginning at the seam line, stitch a ¼" seam to the opposite side, stopping at the seam line.

8. Repeat Steps 6–7, but leave a 3" opening in the middle of the slice/ peel unit.

9. Turn right side out, pushing out the tips of the peel, and fill firmly with polyfill.

10. Hand stitch the 3" opening closed using a whipstitch.

Attaching the Leaf

1. Referring to the embroidery line on the Leaf Template (see page 87), backstitch (Fig. 7) to embroider the veins into the leaf.

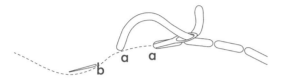

Figure 7

2. Place the embroidered leaf onto the embellished slice, covering the place where the ends of the White bias tape meet and covering the loop seam. Attach, being sure to keep stitches hidden and not to go through the top of the felt. Just a few tacking stitches will do.

3. Stick pins in the slice and sewing needles in the leaf, and you're all done!

Sliced Pincushion Templates

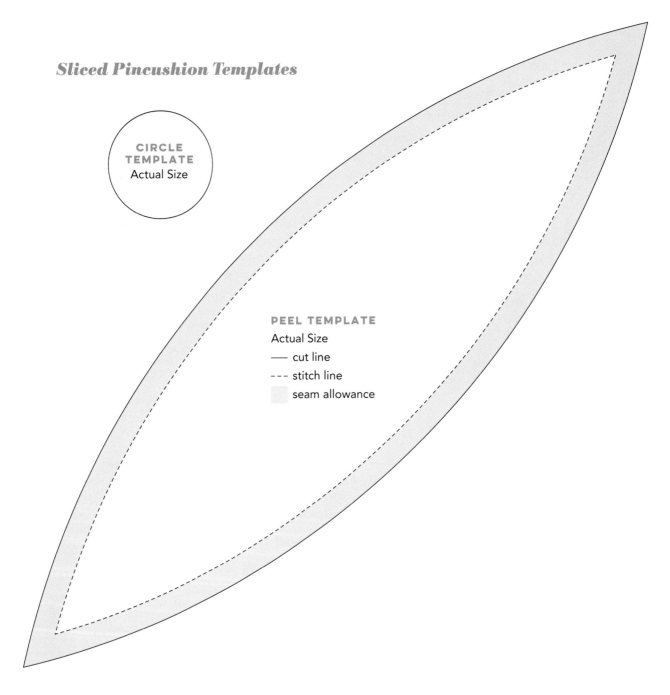

**CIRCLE
TEMPLATE**
Actual Size

PEEL TEMPLATE
Actual Size
—— cut line
--- stitch line
■ seam allowance

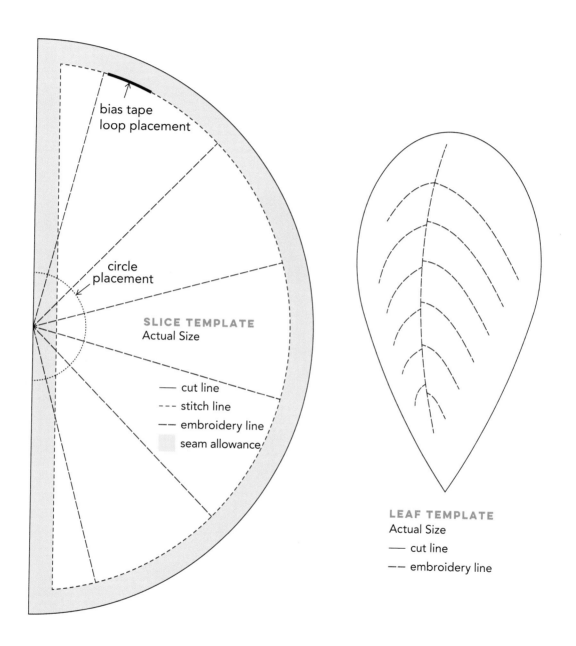

bias tape
loop placement

circle
placement

SLICE TEMPLATE
Actual Size

—— cut line
- - - stitch line
– – embroidery line
⬛ seam allowance

LEAF TEMPLATE
Actual Size
—— cut line
– – embroidery line

CLEMENTINE

There's something about a simple and traditional design that I've always loved. While Amish quilts are not usually made with so much white fabric, to me, this quilt has an Amish look to it. The deep tone of the orange against the white background really shows the design of the quilt blocks and would be well-suited in either a traditional or a modern home.

Finished Quilt Size:
63" x 81"

Finished Block Size: 9'' x 9''

Materials
White Fabric: 3½ yards
Orange Fabric: 1¾ yards
Backing Fabric: 5 yards
Binding Fabric: ¾ yard
Batting: 69" x 87"
Water-soluble pen
Clear acrylic ruler

Cutting
From White Fabric, cut:
(7) 9½" x WOF strips
  Subcut (28) 9½" squares
(12) 3½" x WOF strips
  Subcut (12) 3½" squares from one of the strips
(1) 4¾" x WOF strip
  Subcut (6) 4¾" squares

From Orange Fabric, cut:
(15) 3½" x WOF strips
  Subcut (3) 3½" squares from one of the strips
(1) 4¾" x WOF strip
  Subcut (6) 4¾" squares

From Binding Fabric, cut:
(8) 2½" x WOF strips

Assembling 9-Patch Blocks

1. Sew together (2) 3½" White strips and (1) 3½" Orange strip to create a White-Orange-White strip unit measuring 9½" x WOF. Press toward the Orange fabric. Repeat to create a total of 32 strip units.

2. Sew together (2) 3½" Orange strips and (1) 3½" White strip to create an Orange-White-Orange strip unit measuring 9½" x WOF. Press toward the Orange fabric. Repeat to create a total of 64 strip units. (Fig. 1)

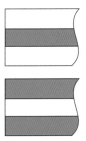

Figure 1

3. Subcut all strip units into 3½" x 9½" rectangles. (Fig. 2)

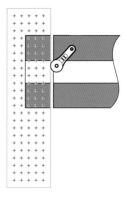

Figure 2

4. Each 9-Patch block will consist of an Orange-White-Orange strip on the top row, a White-Orange-White strip in the middle row, and an Orange-White-Orange strip on the bottom row (Fig. 3).

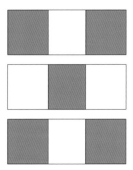

Figure 3

5. Begin by sewing the top row to the middle row; then sew the bottom row to the middle row. Be sure to nest the seams and press between adding each row.

6. Repeat to create a total of (32) 9-Patch blocks.

Assembling the Ohio Star Blocks

1. Using a water-soluble pen and a ruler, draw a diagonal line from corner to corner on the back of each of the six Orange 4¾" squares. (Fig. 4)

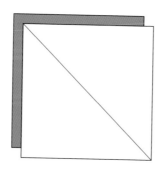

Figure 4

2. With right sides together, pair an Orange 4¾" square with a white 4¾" square.

3. Sew ¼" seams on either side of the drawn line. (Fig. 5)

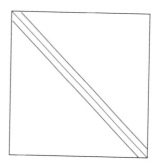

Figure 5

4. Cut along the drawn line to create two Half-Square Triangle (HST) units. (Fig. 6)

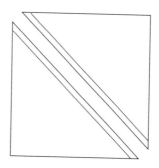

Figure 6

5. With right sides together, combine the two HST units with opposite fabrics matching: Orange with White and White with Orange. (Fig. 7)

6. Draw a line down diagonally from corner to corner, perpendicular to the seam.

7. Sew ¼" seams on either side of drawn line. (Fig. 8)

8. Cut along drawn line.

9. Open block and press seams open.

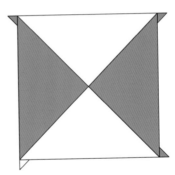

Figure 8

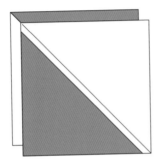

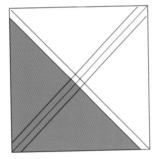

Figure 7

10. Trim and square up the block by lining the center points at the 1¾" mark (Fig. 9). Trim one side. Turn block 90 degrees, line the center points at the 1¾" mark, and trim. Repeat on the other side; then repeat for the last two sides.

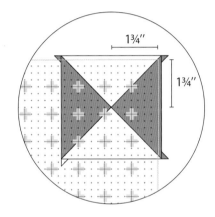

Figure 9

11. Repeat Steps 2–10 to create a total of 12 hourglass units (four hourglass units for each of the three Ohio Star blocks).

12. With right sides together, sew top row: 3½" White square, hourglass block with the Orange hourglass positioned horizontally, 3½" white square (Fig. 10). Press seams.

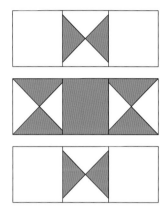

Figure 10

13. With right sides together, sew center row: hourglass block with the Orange hourglass positioned vertically, 3½" Orange square, hourglass block with the Orange hourglass positioned vertically. Press seams.

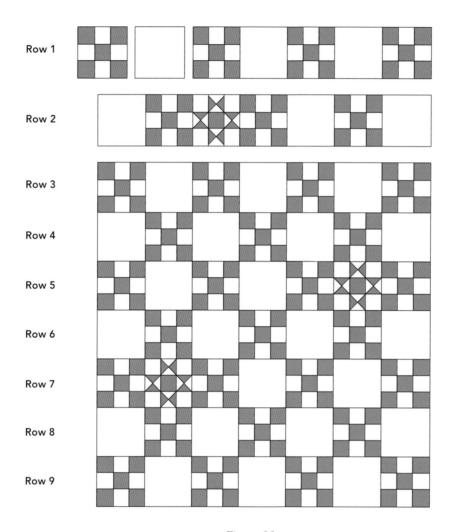

Row 1

Row 2

Row 3

Row 4

Row 5

Row 6

Row 7

Row 8

Row 9

Figure 11

14. With right sides together, sew bottom row: 3½" White square, hourglass block with the Orange hourglass positioned horizontally, 3½" White square. Press seams.

15. With right sides together, sew the top and middle rows together. Complete the block by sewing the bottom row to two top sewn rows. Press the seams.

16. Repeat Steps 12 –15 to create a total of three Ohio Star blocks.

Assembling the Quilt Top

1. Referring to Figure 11, lay out the quilt top's nine rows, each row having seven blocks across, consisting of a combination of 9-Patch blocks, Ohio Star blocks, and 9½" White squares.

Row 1: 9-Patch, White square, 9-Patch, White square, 9-Patch, White square, 9-Patch.

Row 2: White square, 9-Patch, Ohio Star, 9-Patch, White square, 9-Patch, White square.

Row 3: Repeat Row 1.

Row 4: White square, 9-Patch, White square, 9-Patch, White square, 9-Patch, White square.

Row 5: 9-Patch, White square, 9-Patch, White square, 9-Patch, Ohio Star, 9-Patch.

Row 6: Repeat Row 4.

Row 7: 9-Patch, Ohio Star, 9-Patch, White square, 9-Patch, White square, 9-Patch.

Row 8: Repeat Row 4.

Row 9: Repeat Row 1.

2. Sew and press each row.

3. With right sides together, join the rows. Press.

Finishing

1. Layer with the batting and backing, baste, and quilt as desired.

2. Attach the binding using your favorite method.

ACKNOWLEDGMENTS

I am always in awe of the support and love my husband gives me. He's my biggest cheerleader, and best friend, and sometimes willing to give me a little extra nudge I didn't even ask for to get me to push myself a little farther than I normally would. I'm eternally grateful for him and our children. They are my rock and the main reason that I am who I am and why I do what I do. Of course, there are a few great friends who I've been able to bounce ideas off and that I asked to help me with sewing trial runs of projects. To each of them, I thank you from the bottom of my heart for your support and help. I would also like to thank Moda fabrics who supplied fabric for the projects in this book and cheered me on from the get-go. Thank you also to Robert Kaufman, Andover, and Frond for supplying additional fabrics and to Felicia Graves who did all of the quilting in this book. Of course, thank you to Susanne, for her drive, her talent, and her vision. I appreciate your insight and support of this project. I'm grateful for the Lucky Spool Media team that helped to polish and package the book into a beautiful work of art. I am so blessed both within and outside of the quilting industry and this book is a product of all the love and support I receive in my life.

Vanessa Christenson is a blogger, quilter, and pattern designer who is well- known for her original sense of style and unique take on traditional motifs. Vanessa began blogging while her husband was deployed as a means of keeping in touch, but it wasn't long before others started to take notice of the projects she was making. One of the first opportunities offered to her was to participate as a Chef for the Moda Bake Shop website, sponsored by Moda Fabrics. Since then, her designs have been featured in numerous magazines, including: Stitch Magazine, Quilty Magazine, Quilts and More, and Fons and Porter's Love of Quilting. She is the author of the highly rated book *Make it Sew Modern* and has contributed quilt designs to numerous compilation books. Vanessa is an in-demand public speaker and has also been featured on television and web based media outlets, such as: Quilting Arts with Pokey Bolton, Fons and Porter: Love of Quilting, and Craftsy. Over the years, Vanessa's relationship with Moda Fabrics continued to grow and it was through them that she released

her wildly successful first fabric line and Aurifil thread collection, Simply Color, in 2012. She recently released her fourth fabric line and there are more on the way. In addition to all of her other activities, Vanessa is also a BERNINA Ambassador and contributor to the We All Sew blog sponsored by BERNINA. Although she has found immense success in quilting, fabrics, and pattern design, Vanessa is quick to point out that her most important role is as a wife and as a mother to their four children. Vanessa's designs, projects, and patterns can be found on her website, www.vchristenson.com.